# Maximizing Revenue Streams for Assisted Living Owners

*Diversification and Expansion Opportunities*

Dawood Kokawala

Copyright © 2024 Dawood Kokawala

All rights reserved.

No part of this publication may be reproduced, stored or transmitted in any form or by any means, electronic, mechanical, photocopying, recording, scanning, or otherwise without written permission from the publisher. It is illegal to copy this book, post it to a website, or distribute it by any other means without permission.

# Table of Contents

Author's Note ........................................................................ 4

Introduction ......................................................................... 5

**Section 1**

Understanding Revenue Streams in Assisted Living Facilities 7

**Section 2**

Assessing Current Revenue Streams ......................................... 13

**Section 3**

Exploring Diversification Opportunities................................... 22

**Section 4**

Expansion Strategies for Growth............................................... 29

**Section 5**

Financial Planning for Diversification and Expansion............ 38

Conclusion ............................................................................ 51

Appendix................................................................................ 56

# Author's Note

As the CEO and Director of MSDS ALF Growth Solutions Inc., I have dedicated my career to supporting assisted living facilities in their pursuit of excellence. Through my experience and interactions with facility owners and operators, I've witnessed the challenges they face in maximizing revenue streams, navigating financial complexities, and pursuing sustainable growth.

This book is born out of my passion for empowering assisted living facility owners with the knowledge, strategies, and resources they need to thrive in an ever-changing industry landscape. By sharing insights, best practices, and practical guidance, I aim to equip facility owners with the tools they need to unlock their full potential, enhance resident care, and drive long-term success.

I believe that by embracing innovation, fostering collaboration, and embracing a mindset of continuous improvement, assisted living facilities can overcome challenges, seize opportunities, and make a meaningful impact on the lives of residents and their families. It is my sincere hope that this book serves as a valuable resource and inspiration for facility owners on their journey to achieving financial prosperity and operational excellence.

With warm regards,

Dawood Kokawala
CEO and Director
MSDS ALF Growth Solutions Inc.
Tech and Innovation company for Assisted Living Facilities

# Introduction

Welcome to "Maximizing Revenue Streams and Growth Strategies for Assisted Living Facilities," a comprehensive guidebook designed to empower assisted living facility owners and operators with the knowledge, tools, and strategies needed to thrive in today's dynamic healthcare landscape.

As the demand for senior care continues to rise and industry dynamics evolve, assisted living facilities face unprecedented challenges and opportunities. From maximizing revenue streams and diversifying service offerings to exploring expansion opportunities and navigating financial complexities, facility owners must navigate a complex landscape to achieve long-term success.

In this book, we will explore essential strategies for maximizing revenue streams, enhancing resident care, and pursuing sustainable growth. From the importance of financial planning and risk management to the role of innovation and technology in driving operational excellence, each chapter provides practical insights, actionable recommendations, and real-world examples to guide facility owners on their journey to success.

Whether you're a seasoned industry professional or a newcomer to the world of assisted living, this book is designed to be a valuable resource and companion on your path to achieving financial prosperity and operational excellence. Let's embark on this journey together and unlock the full potential of your assisted living facility.

# Section 1

# Understanding Revenue Streams in Assisted Living Facilities

Assisted living facilities rely on various revenue streams to sustain operations and provide quality care to residents. Understanding these revenue streams is essential for owners and operators to manage finances and ensure long-term sustainability effectively.

## 1.1 Overview of Revenue Streams

Understanding the landscape of revenue streams is fundamental for assisted living facility owners to navigate financial planning effectively, while also prioritizing resident safety and well-being. In this overview, we highlight the significance of integrating safety-centric solutions to enhance both financial sustainability and resident safety.

1. Resident Fees: Resident fees remain a primary revenue stream for assisted living facilities, encompassing charges for accommodation, meals, personal care services, and amenities. By investing in safety-centric

solutions, such as fall prevention technologies provided by "ALF Growth Solutions," facilities can enhance resident safety while indirectly contributing to revenue generation through reduced costs associated with resident incidents and injuries.

2. Government Funding: Assisted living facilities may receive government funding through various programs and subsidies aimed at supporting senior care services. These funding sources may include Medicaid waivers, Veterans Affairs benefits, or state-funded assistance programs. Government funding plays a significant role in subsidizing the cost of care for eligible residents and augmenting revenue streams for the facility.

3. Private Pay Options: In addition to resident fees and government funding, assisted living facilities may offer private pay options for residents who do not qualify for government assistance or prefer to pay out-of-pocket for services. Private pay options may include long-term care insurance, personal savings, or assistance from family members. Understanding the preferences and financial capabilities of residents is essential for offering tailored private pay options that meet their needs and preferences.

4. Ancillary Services: Assisted living facilities may generate additional revenue through ancillary services, such as therapy services, medication management, transportation, or recreational activities. These

supplementary services provide value-added benefits to residents and their families while diversifying revenue streams for the facility. Assessing the demand for ancillary services and pricing them competitively is critical for maximizing revenue potential and enhancing overall service offerings.

5. Community Partnerships: Collaborating with community partners, such as healthcare providers, rehabilitation centers, or senior advocacy organizations, can create opportunities for additional revenue streams through joint programs, referral agreements, or shared services. Building strategic partnerships with community stakeholders expands the facility's network, enhances service capabilities, and opens avenues for generating revenue through collaborative initiatives.

6. Philanthropic Support: Assisted living facilities may also receive philanthropic support from donors, foundations, or charitable organizations dedicated to supporting senior care services. Philanthropic contributions may fund special projects, capital improvements, or resident assistance programs, providing financial support beyond traditional revenue streams. Cultivating relationships with philanthropic partners and demonstrating the facility's impact on the community can attract philanthropic support and enhance financial sustainability.

## 1.2 Importance of Diversification in Revenue Streams

Diversification in revenue streams is essential for assisted living facility owners to mitigate risks, enhance financial stability, and adapt to changing market conditions. By diversifying revenue sources, facilities can reduce dependence on any single source of income and create a resilient financial foundation that supports long-term sustainability and growth.

1. Risk Mitigation: Diversification in revenue streams helps mitigate the impact of external factors and market fluctuations on facility finances. By spreading revenue across multiple sources, facilities can reduce their exposure to risks associated with changes in resident demographics, regulatory changes, economic downturns, or industry disruptions. This diversification strategy creates a buffer against revenue volatility and enhances the facility's ability to withstand unforeseen challenges.

2. Enhanced Financial Stability: Diversifying revenue streams enhances financial stability by creating a more balanced and sustainable income portfolio. Instead of relying solely on resident fees or government funding, facilities can generate income from a variety of sources, such as ancillary services, community partnerships, or philanthropic support. This diversified revenue base provides a stable income stream that supports ongoing

operations, facility improvements, and strategic initiatives, even in challenging economic environments.

3. Expansion Opportunities: Diversification opens up opportunities for expansion and growth by tapping into new market segments, service offerings, or geographic locations. By exploring alternative revenue streams, facilities can identify untapped market opportunities, address unmet needs, and diversify their customer base. This strategic approach to revenue diversification enables facilities to expand their reach, increase market share, and capture new sources of revenue that align with their mission and goals.

4. Incorporating innovative solutions such as <u>"ALF Growth Solutions"</u> facilitates this expansion and growth strategy. By leveraging advanced safety-centric technologies and expertise, facilities can not only enhance their existing service offerings but also explore new avenues for revenue generation. "ALF Growth Solutions" provides cutting-edge solutions that empower facilities to differentiate themselves in the market, attract new residents, and expand their reach to previously untapped demographics. Whether it's implementing state-of-the-art fall prevention technologies or offering personalized safety monitoring services, "ALF Growth Solutions" enables facilities to innovate and excel in providing high-quality care while driving sustainable growth and success.

5. Resident-Centric Approach: Diversifying revenue streams allows facilities to tailor services and offerings to meet the diverse needs and preferences of residents. By offering a range of services, amenities, and payment options, facilities can accommodate different resident demographics, income levels, and lifestyle preferences. This resident-centric approach enhances resident satisfaction, improves retention rates, and strengthens the facility's reputation as a provider of high-quality care and services.

6. Innovation and Differentiation: Diversification encourages innovation and differentiation by fostering creativity and experimentation in revenue generation strategies. Facilities can explore innovative service offerings, partnership opportunities, or business models that set them apart from competitors and attract residents and families seeking unique value propositions. This culture of innovation and differentiation drives continuous improvement, stimulates growth, and positions facilities as leaders in the senior care industry.

# Section 2

# Assessing Current Revenue Streams

Assessing the performance and stability of current revenue streams is crucial for assisted living facility owners, ensuring both financial viability and the safety of their residents. As part of this assessment, owners should consider how technology-driven and safety-centric solutions, such as "ALF Growth Solutions," can provide valuable insights and support for revenue optimization efforts.

## 2.1 Conducting a Comprehensive Revenue Stream Analysis

In addition to traditional financial metrics, assisted living facility owners should conduct a comprehensive analysis of revenue streams, considering factors beyond financial performance alone. This analysis encompasses various aspects of resident well-being and operational efficiency, with a focus on enhancing both revenue generation and resident safety.

1. Financial Metrics: Owners should analyze traditional financial metrics such as revenue, expenses, and profit

margins to assess the financial health of the facility. This analysis helps identify revenue streams that are performing well and areas where improvement is needed to optimize financial performance.

2. Resident Satisfaction: Beyond financial metrics, owners should also consider resident satisfaction levels as a key indicator of revenue stream performance. Surveys, feedback mechanisms, and resident engagement initiatives can provide valuable insights into the quality of services provided and the overall satisfaction levels of residents.

3. Operational Efficiency: Assessing the operational efficiency of revenue-generating activities is crucial for maximizing revenue streams. Owners should evaluate processes, workflows, and resource utilization to identify inefficiencies and areas for improvement. Streamlining operations can lead to cost savings, increased productivity, and enhanced revenue generation potential.

4. Safety and Well-being: Importantly, owners should prioritize resident safety and well-being in their revenue stream analysis. Solutions like "ALF Growth Solutions," which specialize in leveraging technology to prevent falls and injuries in Assisted Living Facilities, contribute to a safer living environment and indirectly support revenue growth by reducing costs associated with resident incidents and injuries.

5. Regulatory Compliance: Compliance with regulatory requirements is essential for maintaining revenue streams and avoiding penalties or legal issues. Owners should ensure that revenue-generating activities adhere to relevant regulations and standards, including those related to resident safety, health, and care quality.

## 2.2 Leveraging Technology and Safety-Centric Solutions

In today's rapidly evolving landscape, assisted living facility owners are increasingly turning to technology and safety-centric solutions to enhance revenue streams while prioritizing resident safety and well-being. These innovative solutions leverage advanced technology and data-driven insights to optimize operations, mitigate risks, and create a safer living environment for residents.

1. Technology Integration: Assisted living facilities are embracing technology integration across various aspects of their operations, from resident care management to facility maintenance and security. Solutions such as electronic health records (EHR) systems, resident monitoring devices, and automated safety alerts leverage technology to streamline processes, improve efficiency, and enhance resident safety.

2. Safety-Centric Approach: Central to the adoption of technology solutions is a safety-centric approach aimed

at preventing falls and injuries among residents. Providers like "ALF Growth Solutions" specialize in offering safety-centric technology solutions tailored to the unique needs of assisted living facilities. These solutions may include smart sensors, wearable devices, and predictive analytics tools that detect potential hazards, monitor resident activity, and proactively intervene to prevent accidents.

3. Data-Driven Insights: Technology solutions generate vast amounts of data that can be leveraged to gain valuable insights into facility operations and resident well-being. By analyzing data on resident behavior, health metrics, and facility utilization patterns, owners can identify trends, anticipate needs, and make informed decisions to optimize revenue streams and enhance resident satisfaction.

4. Remote Monitoring and Management: Remote monitoring and management capabilities empower facility staff to oversee operations and respond to emergencies effectively, even from a distance. Solutions like remote access control systems, video surveillance, and real-time communication platforms enable staff to monitor resident activity, address safety concerns, and coordinate response efforts promptly, enhancing overall safety and security.

5. Training and Support: Implementing technology solutions requires proper training and ongoing support

to ensure effective implementation and utilization. Providers like "ALF Growth Solutions" offer comprehensive training programs and technical support services to assist facility staff in leveraging technology effectively, maximizing the benefits of these solutions, and enhancing resident safety and well-being.

## 2.3 Identifying Areas for Improvement

Guided by the results of the revenue stream analysis, assisted living facility owners embark on the task of identifying areas for improvement to optimize revenue generation and enhance resident well-being. This process involves a comprehensive assessment of various aspects of facility operations, service offerings, and safety measures to identify opportunities for enhancement and strategic intervention.

1. Maximizing Occupancy: One key area for improvement is maximizing occupancy rates within the facility. Owners can implement targeted marketing strategies, such as digital advertising campaigns, referral programs, and community outreach initiatives, to attract new residents and improve occupancy levels. Additionally, optimizing resident retention efforts through personalized care plans, social activities, and amenities can help maintain high occupancy rates and minimize revenue loss due to vacancies.

2. Enhancing Service Offerings: Owners should continuously evaluate and enhance service offerings to meet the evolving needs and preferences of residents. This may involve introducing new amenities, such as fitness programs, recreational activities, or dining options, that appeal to residents and differentiate the facility from competitors. By enhancing service offerings, owners can improve resident satisfaction levels, attract new residents, and generate additional revenue streams through fee-based services.

3. Streamlining Operations: Identifying and addressing inefficiencies in facility operations is essential for optimizing revenue generation and maximizing profitability. Owners should evaluate various operational processes, including staffing levels, resource allocation, and administrative tasks, to identify areas for streamlining and improvement. Implementing technology solutions, such as automated scheduling systems, electronic documentation platforms, and workflow optimization tools, can help streamline operations, reduce administrative burdens, and enhance overall efficiency.

4. Safety and Risk Management: Prioritizing resident safety and risk management is paramount for maintaining a secure living environment and minimizing potential liabilities. Owners should conduct regular safety assessments, implement

preventive maintenance programs, and provide ongoing staff training on safety protocols and emergency procedures. Additionally, leveraging technology-driven safety solutions, such as fall detection systems, emergency call systems, and surveillance cameras, can help mitigate risks, prevent accidents, and enhance resident safety within the facility.

## 2.4 Planning for Future Growth with a Focus on Safety

In envisioning future growth, assisted living facility owners embark on a strategic journey aimed at expanding operations, enhancing services, and ensuring the continued well-being of residents. This planning process involves careful consideration of market trends, resident needs, regulatory requirements, and safety considerations to chart a course for sustainable growth and long-term success.

1. Setting Strategic Objectives: The first step in planning for future growth is setting clear and achievable strategic objectives aligned with the facility's mission and vision. These objectives may include increasing occupancy rates, expanding service offerings, improving operational efficiency, or entering new market segments. By defining specific goals and timelines, owners provide a roadmap for guiding growth initiatives and measuring progress over time.

2. <u>Market Analysis and Opportunity Identification</u>:

   Conducting a comprehensive market analysis is essential for identifying growth opportunities and understanding the competitive landscape. Owners should assess demographic trends, demand for assisted living services, competitor offerings, and regulatory changes to identify untapped market segments or emerging opportunities. This analysis informs strategic decisions regarding target markets, service differentiation, and expansion strategies.

3. Financial Planning and Resource Allocation: Effective financial planning is critical for supporting growth initiatives and ensuring the availability of resources to execute strategic objectives. Owners should develop detailed financial projections, including revenue forecasts, expense budgets, and capital investment plans. By aligning financial resources with growth priorities, owners can allocate funds strategically, prioritize investments, and optimize resource utilization for maximum impact.

4. Risk Assessment and Mitigation Strategies: Assessing potential risks and developing mitigation strategies is essential for safeguarding against unforeseen challenges that may impact growth initiatives. Owners should identify internal and external risks, such as regulatory changes, economic downturns, or competitive pressures, and develop contingency plans

to mitigate their impact. By proactively addressing risks, owners can minimize disruptions and maintain momentum toward achieving growth objectives.

5. Collaboration and Partnerships: Collaborating with strategic partners and industry stakeholders can accelerate growth initiatives and enhance the facility's competitive position. Owners should explore partnership opportunities with healthcare providers, technology vendors, community organizations, and other stakeholders to leverage resources, access expertise, and explore new avenues for growth. Collaborative partnerships can provide access to specialized services, innovative solutions, and new market opportunities, driving sustainable growth and differentiation.

6. Continuous Evaluation and Adaptation: Growth planning is an iterative process that requires continuous evaluation and adaptation to changing market conditions and resident needs. Owners should regularly review progress against strategic objectives, assess the effectiveness of growth initiatives, and adjust strategies as needed. By remaining agile and responsive to market dynamics, owners can optimize growth opportunities, mitigate risks, and ensure the facility's long-term success and sustainability.

# Section 3

# Exploring Diversification Opportunities

In this section, we'll explore various strategies that assisted living owners can use to diversify their revenue streams. We'll provide detailed explanations of each strategy, along with real-world examples or case studies to illustrate how other facilities have successfully implemented them. Additionally, we'll discuss the potential benefits and challenges associated with each diversification opportunity, helping owners make informed decisions about which strategies are most suitable for their facility

## 3.1 Introducing New Services or Amenities

Introducing new services or amenities is a proactive approach to diversifying revenue streams and meeting the evolving needs of residents. Assisted living facilities can identify opportunities for innovation and differentiation by introducing value-added services that enhance resident experiences and attract new clientele.

1. Identifying Opportunities: Facilities can conduct market research, resident surveys, and needs assessments to identify areas where new services or amenities could address unmet needs or preferences. For example, there may be demand for specialized wellness programs, personalized care services, or innovative recreational activities that cater to specific resident demographics or lifestyle preferences.

2. Developing Innovative Offerings: Once opportunities have been identified, facilities can develop innovative offerings that differentiate them from competitors and create additional revenue streams. This may involve partnering with healthcare professionals, wellness experts, or technology providers to design and implement unique programs or services that promote resident well-being and enhance quality of life.

3. Marketing and Promotion: Effectively marketing new services or amenities is essential for generating awareness and attracting resident interest. Facilities can utilize various marketing channels, such as social media, email newsletters, and community events, to promote their offerings and showcase the value they provide to residents and their families.

**Example:**

"ABC Assisted Living Facility successfully introduced a new fall prevention program in partnership with 'ALF Growth Solutions.' Leveraging advanced safety-centric technologies, including smart sensors and wearable devices, the program provides personalized fall risk assessments, monitoring, and intervention strategies to residents. By implementing this innovative program, ABC Assisted Living Facility not only prioritizes resident safety but also creates a unique selling point that attracts new residents and enhances revenue streams."

## 3.2 Partnering with Healthcare Providers or Community Organizations

Collaborating with healthcare providers or community organizations presents valuable opportunities for assisted living facilities to diversify their revenue streams and expand their service offerings. By establishing strategic partnerships, facilities can leverage complementary expertise, resources, and networks to enhance resident care, attract new clientele, and drive revenue growth.

1. Identifying Synergistic Partnerships: Assisted living facilities can identify potential healthcare providers or community organizations with complementary services, missions, or target demographics. These partnerships may include healthcare systems, rehabilitation centers, home health agencies, senior

centers, or advocacy groups that share a common goal of promoting senior health and well-being.

2. Establishing Collaborative Initiatives: Once suitable partners have been identified, facilities can explore collaborative initiatives that leverage each partner's strengths and resources. This may involve co-developing specialized care programs, coordinating care transitions, or facilitating referrals between healthcare providers and assisted living facilities. By working together, partners can provide comprehensive care solutions that address the holistic needs of seniors and their families.

3. Expanding Referral Networks: Partnering with healthcare providers or community organizations expands referral networks and access to potential residents. Facilities can benefit from referrals from hospitals, physician practices, rehabilitation centers, or social service agencies, increasing occupancy rates and revenue opportunities. Likewise, healthcare partners can refer patients or clients to assisted living facilities for ongoing care, rehabilitation, or transitional support, creating mutually beneficial relationships.

**Example:**
"XYZ Assisted Living Facility established a strategic partnership with Regional Medical Center to enhance post-acute care transitions for seniors. Through this partnership, XYZ Assisted Living Facility receives referrals for patients

transitioning from hospital to home, providing personalized rehabilitation services, medication management, and follow-up care. In return, Regional Medical Center benefits from streamlined care transitions, reduced readmission rates, and improved patient outcomes. This collaborative initiative not only strengthens relationships with healthcare providers but also diversifies revenue streams and enhances resident care."

## 3.3 Developing Ancillary Income Sources

Developing ancillary income sources offers assisted living facilities additional avenues for revenue diversification and business expansion. By leveraging their expertise, resources, and infrastructure, facilities can create supplementary income streams that complement their core services and contribute to financial sustainability.

1. Identifying Ancillary Income Opportunities: Assisted living facilities can identify ancillary income opportunities based on their unique strengths, capabilities, and market demand. These opportunities may include offering consulting services, training programs, or specialized care services that leverage the facility's expertise and resources. Facilities can also explore creative ways to monetize existing assets or services, such as renting out space for events or providing fee-based concierge services.

2. Developing Value-Added Services: Once ancillary income opportunities have been identified, facilities can

develop value-added services that meet the needs of their target audience and differentiate them from competitors. This may involve creating consulting packages tailored to specific client needs, designing training programs for staff or external stakeholders, or offering premium services that enhance resident experiences and satisfaction.

3. Marketing and Promotion: Effectively marketing ancillary income sources is essential for generating awareness and attracting clients. Facilities can utilize various marketing channels, such as professional networks, industry associations, and digital platforms, to promote their services and showcase the value they provide. Case studies, testimonials, and client success stories can also help demonstrate the benefits of ancillary income sources and attract new clients.

**Example**:
"Sunrise Assisted Living Facility developed a series of caregiver training workshops in partnership with 'ALF Growth Solutions.' Leveraging their expertise in senior care and safety, Sunrise Assisted Living Facility offers comprehensive training programs for family caregivers, healthcare professionals, and community members. These workshops cover topics such as fall prevention, dementia care, and medication management, providing valuable education and support to caregivers while generating ancillary income for the facility. By offering these value-added services, Sunrise

Assisted Living Facility strengthens its position as a leader in senior care and diversifies its revenue streams."

# Section 4

# Expansion Strategies for Growth

In Section 4, we'll discuss various expansion opportunities for assisted living facilities, including opening additional locations or satellite facilities, expanding service offerings to include memory care and specialized care, and targeting new markets or demographics. We'll highlight the benefits and potential challenges associated with each expansion strategy, providing insights to help assisted-living facility owners make informed decisions about their growth initiatives.

## 4.1 Opening Additional Locations or Satellite Facilities

Expanding through the opening of additional locations or satellite facilities is a strategic growth initiative for assisted living facilities seeking to extend their reach and serve a larger population of seniors. This expansion strategy offers various benefits but also presents challenges that require careful consideration and planning.

**Benefits of Opening Additional Locations:**

1. Increased Market Penetration: Opening additional locations allows assisted living facilities to expand their geographic footprint and reach new markets. By strategically selecting locations with high demand and favorable demographics, facilities can increase their market penetration and attract a larger customer base.

2. Economies of Scale: Operating multiple locations enables facilities to achieve economies of scale through centralized management, shared resources, and bulk purchasing. This can result in cost savings, improved efficiency, and enhanced profitability for each facility.

3. Enhanced Brand Visibility: Establishing a presence in multiple locations enhances brand visibility and recognition within the community. This can strengthen the facility's reputation, attract prospective residents and their families, and create opportunities for word-of-mouth referrals.

**Potential Challenges:**

1. Regulatory Compliance: Opening additional locations requires compliance with state and local regulations governing assisted living facilities. Facilities must navigate licensing requirements, zoning ordinances, and building codes to ensure legal and regulatory compliance at each location.

2. Staffing Shortages: Recruiting and retaining qualified staff members can be challenging, especially when expanding to new locations. Facilities must have robust recruitment strategies, training programs, and retention initiatives in place to address staffing shortages and maintain quality care standards.

3. Operational Complexities: Managing multiple locations introduces operational complexities, including coordination of services, communication across sites, and standardization of policies and procedures. Facilities must implement effective management systems, technology solutions, and communication channels to streamline operations and ensure consistency across locations.

**Example:**
"Sunrise Assisted Living expanded its operations by opening a satellite facility in a neighboring community with a growing senior population. Leveraging its successful model and brand reputation, Sunrise Assisted Living extended its reach to serve a new market segment while maintaining its commitment to high-quality care and services. By strategically selecting the location, investing in staff training, and implementing robust operational systems, Sunrise Assisted Living successfully navigated the challenges of expansion and established a strong presence in the community."

## 4.2 Expanding Service Offerings

Expanding service offerings to include memory care, specialized care, or other niche services is a strategic approach for assisted living facilities to meet the diverse needs of seniors and differentiate themselves in the market. This expansion strategy offers various benefits but also presents challenges that require careful planning and execution.

## Benefits of Expanding Service Offerings:

1. Attracting New Residents: Expanding service offerings allows facilities to attract new residents with specialized care needs, such as memory care for individuals with Alzheimer's disease or dementia. By providing comprehensive care solutions that address specific health conditions or care requirements, facilities can appeal to a broader demographic and increase occupancy rates.

2. Increasing Revenue Potential: Offering additional services creates opportunities for revenue diversification and growth. Memory care, specialized care, and other niche services often command higher fees or reimbursement rates, contributing to increased revenue streams and financial sustainability for the facility. Additionally, value-added services such as safety-centric technologies provided by "ALF Growth Solutions" can further enhance revenue potential by

attracting residents and families seeking innovative care solutions.

3. Improving Resident Outcomes: Expanding service offerings allows facilities to tailor care plans to meet the unique needs of each resident, resulting in improved health outcomes and quality of life. By providing specialized care services, facilities can address complex medical conditions, promote independence, and enhance the overall well-being of residents. This personalized approach to care not only enhances resident satisfaction but also strengthens the facility's reputation as a provider of high-quality care.

**Potential Challenges:**

1. Staffing Requirements: Expanding service offerings may require additional staffing with specialized training or certifications. Facilities must ensure adequate staffing levels, invest in staff training programs, and recruit qualified professionals to deliver specialized care services effectively.

2. Training Needs: Providing specialized care services necessitates ongoing training and professional development for staff members. Facilities must invest in training programs, continuing education opportunities, and certifications to ensure staff competency and compliance with industry standards and regulations.

3. Operational Adjustments: Expanding service offerings introduces operational complexities, including adjustments to care delivery processes, infrastructure requirements, and administrative procedures. Facilities must develop effective operational systems, protocols, and communication channels to support the delivery of specialized care services and maintain quality standards across the organization.

**Example:**
"Harmony Assisted Living Facility expanded its service offerings to include memory care services for residents with Alzheimer's disease and related dementias. Partnering with 'ALF Growth Solutions,' Harmony Assisted Living Facility implemented advanced safety-centric technologies, such as smart sensors and monitoring systems, to enhance resident safety and well-being. By offering specialized memory care services supported by innovative technology solutions, Harmony Assisted Living Facility differentiated itself in the market and attracted residents and families seeking comprehensive care and peace of mind."

Expanding service offerings to include memory care, specialized care, or other niche services presents opportunities for assisted living facilities to attract new residents, increase revenue potential, and improve resident outcomes. However, facilities must address staffing requirements, training needs, and operational adjustments to ensure successful implementation and sustainable growth.

## 4.3 Targeting New Markets or Demographics

Targeting new markets or demographics presents assisted living facilities with valuable opportunities for growth and expansion. By identifying underserved populations or emerging trends in senior living preferences, facilities can adapt their offerings and marketing strategies to attract a diverse clientele. However, this expansion strategy also entails challenges that require careful consideration and planning.

**Benefits of Targeting New Markets or Demographics:**

1. Increased Demand: Targeting new markets or demographics allows assisted living facilities to tap into the growing demand for senior care services. This may include targeting specific demographic groups, such as baby boomers, ethnic minorities, or LGBTQ+ seniors, who have unique needs or preferences that are not adequately addressed by existing facilities.

2. Higher Occupancy Rates: By catering to underserved populations or niche market segments, facilities can achieve higher occupancy rates and maximize revenue potential. By offering culturally sensitive services, language-specific programming, or specialized care options, facilities can attract residents who may otherwise be reluctant to consider assisted living as a viable option.

3. Competitive Advantage: Targeting new markets or demographics enables facilities to differentiate

themselves from competitors and establish a competitive advantage in the marketplace. By offering innovative services, amenities, or programming tailored to the needs and preferences of specific demographic groups, facilities can position themselves as leaders in senior care and attract residents seeking personalized solutions.

**Potential Challenges:**

1. Cultural Sensitivity: Targeting new demographics requires cultural sensitivity and awareness of diverse needs, beliefs, and traditions. Facilities must ensure that their offerings are inclusive, respectful, and responsive to the cultural backgrounds and preferences of residents and their families.

2. Marketing Strategies: Effectively reaching and engaging new markets or demographics requires tailored marketing strategies and messaging. Facilities must invest in market research, demographic analysis, and targeted advertising to identify key influencers, channels, and communication platforms for reaching their target audience.

3. Regulatory Considerations: Targeting new markets or demographics may involve navigating regulatory considerations, such as language access requirements, cultural competency standards, or compliance with diversity and inclusion initiatives. Facilities must stay

abreast of regulatory requirements and best practices for serving diverse populations to ensure legal compliance and ethical standards.

**Example:**

"Golden Age Assisted Living Facility identified a growing need for culturally sensitive senior care services within the Hispanic community in their area. In response, Golden Age Assisted Living Facility developed a bilingual staff training program, Spanish-language programming, and culturally themed activities to better serve Hispanic residents and their families. By tailoring their offerings to meet the unique needs and preferences of the Hispanic community, Golden Age Assisted Living Facility achieved higher occupancy rates and strengthened its reputation as a provider of inclusive and culturally competent care."

Targeting new markets or demographics presents opportunities for assisted living facilities to expand their customer base, increase occupancy rates, and establish a competitive advantage. However, facilities must address challenges related to cultural sensitivity, marketing strategies, and regulatory considerations to ensure successful expansion and sustainable growth.

# Section 5

# Financial Planning for Diversification and Expansion

In Section 5, we'll provide practical guidance on financial planning for assisted living facilities looking to diversify their revenue streams and expand their operations. This section will cover budgeting, financial forecasting, risk management, securing funding or financing, and include expert insights or advice from industry professionals.

## 5.1 Budgeting for Diversification and Expansion

Effective budgeting is essential for assisted living facilities embarking on diversification and expansion initiatives. A well-designed budget serves as a roadmap for allocating financial resources, setting priorities, and achieving strategic goals. In this section, we'll offer practical guidance and strategies for creating comprehensive budgets that support diversification and expansion efforts.

## Identifying Revenue and Expense Categories:

Assisted living facilities should start by identifying and categorizing revenue and expense items relevant to their diversification and expansion plans. Revenue categories may include resident fees, ancillary income, grants, and fundraising revenue. Expense categories may include staffing costs, facility maintenance, technology investments, marketing expenses, and regulatory compliance costs.

## Allocating Resources Effectively:

Once revenue and expense categories have been identified, facilities should allocate resources effectively to support diversification and expansion initiatives. This involves prioritizing investments based on strategic objectives, anticipated returns, and resource constraints. Facilities should consider factors such as market demand, competitive dynamics, regulatory requirements, and operational capacity when allocating resources to different initiatives.

## Setting Realistic Financial Goals:

Setting realistic financial goals is crucial for ensuring that diversification and expansion initiatives are financially viable and sustainable. Facilities should establish clear, measurable objectives for revenue growth, expense management, profitability, and return on investment. These goals should be aligned with the facility's overall mission, vision, and strategic priorities, taking into account market trends, competitive pressures, and internal capabilities.

**Monitoring and Reviewing Performance:**

Regular monitoring and review of financial performance are essential for tracking progress, identifying variances, and making informed decisions. Facilities should establish key performance indicators (KPIs) and metrics to measure the success of diversification and expansion initiatives, such as occupancy rates, revenue growth, expense ratios, and profitability margins. Ongoing review of financial performance enables facilities to adjust strategies, reallocate resources, and address emerging challenges or opportunities.

**Example:**

"Sunrise Assisted Living Facility developed a comprehensive budget to support its diversification and expansion into memory care services. By carefully identifying revenue and expense categories, allocating resources effectively, and setting realistic financial goals, Sunrise Assisted Living Facility was able to successfully launch its memory care program while maintaining financial stability. Regular monitoring and review of financial performance allowed the facility to track progress, identify areas for improvement, and make adjustments as needed to achieve its strategic objectives."

## 5.2 Financial Forecasting

Financial forecasting plays a crucial role in the success of diversification and expansion initiatives for assisted living facilities. By predicting future financial performance and assessing the feasibility of strategic plans, facilities can make informed decisions, allocate resources effectively, and mitigate risks. In this section, we'll explore various techniques and considerations for conducting financial forecasting in the context of diversification and expansion.

**Revenue Projections:**

Assisted living facilities should start by forecasting revenue projections for new services, markets, or demographics targeted through diversification and expansion initiatives. This involves estimating potential revenue streams based on factors such as pricing strategies, market demand, occupancy rates, and competitive dynamics. Facilities may use historical data, market research, industry benchmarks, and input from stakeholders to inform revenue projections.

**Expense Analysis:**

In addition to revenue projections, facilities should conduct a thorough analysis of expenses associated with diversification and expansion initiatives. This includes identifying and estimating costs related to staffing, facility upgrades, technology investments, marketing campaigns, regulatory compliance, and other operational expenses. Facilities should consider both one-time expenses and ongoing operational costs when forecasting expenses.

**Sensitivity Analysis:**

Sensitivity analysis involves assessing the impact of various external factors, assumptions, and scenarios on financial forecasts. Assisted living facilities should conduct sensitivity analysis to evaluate the potential effects of changes in key variables, such as occupancy rates, pricing structures, reimbursement rates, and market conditions, on the financial performance of diversification and expansion initiatives. This allows facilities to identify potential risks, uncertainties, and opportunities and develop contingency plans accordingly.

**Scenario Planning:**

Scenario planning involves creating multiple financial scenarios based on different assumptions, outcomes, and market conditions. Assisted living facilities should develop best-case, worst-case, and most likely scenarios to assess the range of possible outcomes for diversification and expansion initiatives. This helps facilities anticipate potential challenges, adapt to changing circumstances, and make proactive decisions to optimize financial performance and mitigate risks.

**Example:**
"Golden Age Assisted Living Facility conducted financial forecasting to assess the feasibility of expanding its service offerings to include specialized memory care services. By projecting potential revenue streams, estimating expenses, and conducting sensitivity analysis, Golden Age Assisted Living Facility identified various scenarios and associated risks. This enabled the facility to develop a strategic plan that optimized resource allocation, minimized financial risks, and maximized the potential for success."

## 5.3 Risk Management

Risk management is a critical aspect of financial planning for diversification and expansion initiatives in assisted living facilities. By identifying, assessing, and mitigating financial risks, facilities can safeguard their financial health, protect against potential losses, and ensure the success of strategic initiatives. In this section, we'll explore key principles and strategies for effective risk management in the context of diversification and expansion, including the role of safety-centric technology solutions like "[ALF Growth Solutions](#)."

**Identifying Financial Risks:**

Assisted living facilities should start by identifying potential financial risks associated with diversification and expansion initiatives. These risks may include market volatility, regulatory changes, competitive pressures, operational challenges, staffing shortages, technology disruptions, and unforeseen events such as natural disasters or pandemics. Facilities should conduct a thorough risk assessment to identify and prioritize risks based on their likelihood and potential impact on financial performance.

**Assessing Risk Exposure:**

Once financial risks have been identified, facilities should assess their exposure to each risk and its potential impact on financial outcomes. This involves quantifying the magnitude of potential losses, evaluating the probability of occurrence, and determining the level of risk tolerance for the facility.

Facilities may use risk assessment tools, models, or frameworks to systematically evaluate and prioritize risks based on their severity and significance.

## Mitigating Risks with "ALF Growth Solutions":

As part of their risk mitigation strategies, assisted living facilities can leverage safety-centric technology solutions like "ALF Growth Solutions" to address operational challenges and enhance resident safety. By implementing smart sensors, monitoring systems, and other innovative technologies, facilities can proactively identify and mitigate risks related to falls, injuries, wandering, and other safety concerns. These solutions provide real-time data and alerts, enabling staff to respond promptly to potential emergencies and prevent adverse events.

## Contingency Planning:

Despite proactive risk mitigation efforts, assisted living facilities should prepare for the possibility of unforeseen events or adverse outcomes. Contingency planning involves developing response plans, alternative strategies, and emergency protocols to address potential risks and minimize disruptions to operations. Facilities should establish communication channels, escalation procedures, and crisis management protocols to effectively respond to unexpected challenges and protect financial stability.

**Example:**

"Silver Springs Assisted Living Facility partnered with 'ALF Growth Solutions' to enhance its risk management efforts and improve resident safety. By installing smart sensors and monitoring systems throughout the facility, Silver Springs Assisted Living Facility gained real-time insights into resident activity and behavior, allowing staff to proactively address potential safety concerns and prevent accidents. This proactive approach not only minimized the risk of falls and injuries but also enhanced the facility's reputation for providing high-quality care and ensuring resident well-being."

## 5.4 Securing Funding or Financing

Securing funding or financing is often a crucial step in implementing diversification and expansion initiatives for assisted living facilities. Whether it's funding for facility upgrades, new service offerings, or expansion into new markets, having access to adequate financial resources is essential for success. In this section, we'll explore various tips and strategies for securing funding or financing tailored to the unique needs and circumstances of assisted living facilities.

**Understanding Funding Options:**

Assisted living facilities have a range of funding options available to them, including loans, grants, equity financing, and partnerships. Each option has its own advantages and considerations, and facilities should carefully evaluate which option best aligns with their goals, financial situation, and risk tolerance. For example, loans offer immediate access to capital but require repayment with interest, while grants provide non-repayable funds but may be subject to eligibility criteria and competition.

## Building Strong Relationships with Lenders and Investors:

Establishing strong relationships with lenders, investors, and financial institutions is key to accessing funding or financing for diversification and expansion initiatives. Facilities should proactively network with potential lenders and investors, communicate their vision and strategic plans effectively, and demonstrate a track record of financial stability and operational excellence. Building trust and credibility with financial partners can increase the likelihood of securing favorable terms and conditions for funding.

## Preparing a Comprehensive Funding Proposal:

To attract funding or financing, assisted living facilities should prepare a comprehensive funding proposal that outlines their diversification and expansion plans, financial projections, risk management strategies, and potential returns on investment. The proposal should clearly articulate the facility's value proposition, competitive advantage, and growth potential, demonstrating to lenders and investors why they should invest in the facility. Facilities should also be prepared to provide supporting documentation, such as financial statements, business plans, and market research, to substantiate their funding request.

**Exploring Public and Private Funding Sources:**

Assisted living facilities can explore a variety of public and private funding sources to support diversification and expansion initiatives. Public funding sources may include government grants, community development programs, and economic development initiatives aimed at supporting healthcare infrastructure and senior services. Private funding sources may include venture capital firms, private equity investors, and angel investors interested in healthcare and aging-related industries. Facilities should research and evaluate funding opportunities from both the public and private sectors to identify potential sources of capital that align with their strategic objectives.

**Example:**
"Maple Grove Assisted Living Facility successfully secured financing for its expansion into memory care services by partnering with a local community development agency. By leveraging a combination of government grants and low-interest loans, Maple Grove Assisted Living Facility was able to fund facility upgrades, staff training programs, and specialized memory care amenities. This strategic approach to funding not only supported the facility's growth initiatives but also strengthened its relationships with the local community and government stakeholders."

## 5.5 Expert Insights and Advice

In this section, we'll provide expert insights and advice from industry professionals, financial advisors, and business leaders with experience in diversification and expansion strategies for assisted living facilities. These insights offer valuable perspectives, best practices, and actionable recommendations for successful financial planning and execution, including the role of safety-centric technology solutions like "[ALF Growth Solutions](#)."

**Industry Professionals:**

Industry professionals, including senior living consultants, healthcare executives, and facility administrators, can offer valuable insights into the unique challenges and opportunities facing assisted living facilities in today's dynamic healthcare landscape. Their firsthand experience and expertise can inform strategic decision-making, risk management strategies, and operational best practices for diversification and expansion initiatives.

**Financial Advisors:**

Financial advisors specializing in healthcare and senior living can provide tailored advice and guidance on financial planning, budgeting, forecasting, and securing funding for diversification and expansion projects. They can help facilities navigate complex financial considerations, assess investment opportunities, and optimize capital allocation strategies to support growth and sustainability. Financial advisors can also offer insights into industry trends, regulatory changes, and market dynamics affecting assisted living facilities.

## Business Leaders:

Business leaders with experience in diversification, expansion, and innovation can share valuable lessons learned, success stories, and best practices from their entrepreneurial journeys. Their insights into strategic planning, risk management, and organizational leadership can inspire and inform assisted living facilities seeking to expand their service offerings, enter new markets, or adopt innovative technologies like "ALF Growth Solutions." Business leaders can also guide building strategic partnerships, fostering a culture of innovation, and driving sustainable growth in a competitive marketplace.

## Role of "ALF Growth Solutions":

As part of expert insights and advice, the role of safety-centric technology solutions like "ALF Growth Solutions" can be highlighted. Industry professionals and business leaders can discuss the importance of leveraging innovative technologies to enhance resident safety, improve operational efficiency, and differentiate assisted living facilities in the marketplace. By incorporating "ALF Growth Solutions" into their diversification and expansion strategies, facilities can demonstrate their commitment to providing high-quality care, maintaining regulatory compliance, and fostering a culture of innovation and excellence.

**Example:**

"Dr. Sarah Johnson, a senior living consultant with over 20 years of experience in the healthcare industry, emphasizes the importance of adopting innovative technologies like 'ALF Growth Solutions' to enhance resident safety and well-being. According to Dr. Johnson, integrating smart sensors, monitoring systems, and predictive analytics into assisted living facilities can proactively identify potential risks, prevent adverse events, and improve the overall quality of care. By leveraging technology solutions like 'ALF Growth Solutions,' facilities can not only enhance resident satisfaction but also achieve operational efficiencies and drive sustainable growth."

# Conclusion

In this e-book, we've explored essential strategies for assisted living facility owners to maximize their revenue streams, enhance resident care, and pursue sustainable growth. As the senior living landscape continues to evolve, facility owners must take proactive steps to adapt to changing market dynamics and seize opportunities for innovation and expansion.

**Key Takeaways:**

1. Diversification is Key: Diversifying revenue streams through new services, markets, and partnerships can help assisted living facilities mitigate risks, increase profitability, and better meet the diverse needs of residents.

2. Financial Planning is Essential: Effective financial planning, budgeting, and forecasting are essential for supporting diversification and expansion initiatives, ensuring financial stability, and achieving long-term success.

3. Risk Management Matters: Identifying, assessing, and mitigating financial risks is critical for safeguarding the financial health of assisted living facilities and protecting against potential losses.

4. Innovation Drives Growth: Leveraging innovative technologies like "ALF Growth Solutions" can enhance resident safety, improve operational efficiency, and differentiate facilities in the competitive senior living market.

5. Take Proactive Steps:

We encourage assisted living facility owners to take proactive steps to maximize their revenue streams, explore growth opportunities, and enhance the quality of care for residents. By embracing innovation, adopting best practices, and fostering a culture of continuous improvement, facilities can position themselves for long-term success and make a positive impact on the lives of seniors and their families.

# Connect with us

For further assistance or consultation on implementing the strategies discussed in this e-book, including leveraging safety-centric technology solutions like "ALF Growth Solutions," please contact us at info@alfgrowth.health.

Our team of experts is dedicated to supporting assisted living facilities in achieving their financial and operational goals and making a meaningful difference in the lives of residents.

## Join us on Facebook Group

https://www.facebook.com/groups/alfgrowth

# Appendix

**Additional Resources:**

- LeadingAge: LeadingAge is a national association of nonprofit aging services organizations dedicated to advancing policies, promoting practices, and conducting research that supports, enables, and empowers people to live fully as they age. Website: LeadingAge

- Argentum: Argentum is the leading national association exclusively dedicated to supporting companies operating professionally managed, resident-centered senior living communities and the older adults and families they serve. Website: Argentum

- Aging in Place Technology Watch: Aging in Place Technology Watch is an advisory service focused on the market and business of technology-based aging services. The site publishes research, consults, and hosts conferences focused on technology for older adults aging in place. Website: Aging in Place Technology Watch

- Senior Housing News: Senior Housing News is the leading source of news and information covering the senior housing industry. The publication provides in-depth analysis, insights, and trends shaping the future of senior living. Website: Senior Housing News.

## Glossary of Key Terms:

1. Revenue Diversification: Revenue diversification refers to the strategy of generating income from multiple sources, reducing dependence on any single revenue stream.

2. Expansion: Expansion involves increasing the scale, scope, or reach of assisted living facilities through initiatives such as opening new locations, introducing new services, or targeting new markets.

3. Financial Planning: Financial planning is the process of developing strategies to manage financial resources, allocate funds effectively, and achieve long-term financial goals.

4. Risk Management: Risk management involves identifying, assessing, and mitigating financial risks to protect against potential losses and ensure the financial stability of assisted living facilities.

5. Innovation: Innovation refers to the introduction of new ideas, technologies, or processes that drive positive change and improvement in assisted living operations and resident care.

www.ingramcontent.com/pod-product-compliance
Lightning Source LLC
Chambersburg PA
CBHW050244230526
45470CB00005B/2100